Overtures and Preludes

in Full Score

RICHARD WAGNER

DOVER PUBLICATIONS, INC.
Mineola, New York

Bibliographical Note

This Dover edition, first published in 1996, is a new compilation of works originally published in separate editions. *Fünf Vorspiele (Ouvertüren) und Isoldens Liebestod von Richard Wagner* was originally published as Edition Peters No. 9847 by C. F. Peters, Leipzig, n.d.—a collection containing the overtures to *Die Meistersinger* and *Tannhäuser*, the preludes to *Lohengrin*, Act I, and *Parsifal*, and the prelude and "Liebestod" from *Tristan und Isolde*. The overture to *Der fliegende Holländer* was originally published by Adolph Fürstner, Berlin, n.d., edited by Felix Weingartner, and republished in 1988 by Dover Publications, Inc., in *Richard Wagner, The Flying Dutchman in Full Score*. The prelude to *Lohengrin*, Act III, and the overture to *Rienzi* were originally published separately in authoritative early editions; the latter work was edited with playing cues by Fritz Hoffmann.

The Dover edition adds lists of contents and instrumentation, a glossary of German terms and performance notes in the scores, and background information on the libretti, composition and first performances of the works in this volume.

International Standard Book Number: 0-486-29201-0

Manufactured in the United States of America
Dover Publications, Inc., 31 East 2nd Street, Mineola, N.Y. 11501

Contents

Glossary of German Terms
and Score Notes

aber (gut) (sehr) markiert, but (well) (very) marked
aber sehr ausdrucksvoll, but very expressively
a.d.g. (auf der G-Saite), on the G string
allein, alone (solo)
allmählich immer stärker, continuously stronger
allmählich im Zeitmaß etwas zurückhaltend, gradually
   restraining the tempo a bit
an jedem Pulte nur der erste Spieler, the first player only
   at each desk
auf der G-Saite, on the G string
ausdrucksvoll, expressively

belebend, quicken
belebt, animated
bewegt, doch immer noch etwas breit, agitated, yet always
   rather broad
Bog(en) = bowed (*arco*)

Dämpf[er] weg, take off the mute
durch Flageolett hervorzubringen, to be played as harmonics

ein wenig rallent[ando], slightly held back
(4) einzelne Violinen, (4) solo violins
etwas bewegter, somewhat more agitated
etwas gedehnt, rather stretched out
etwas zurückhalten, somewhat held back

feurig, fiery

gebunden = legato
gehalten, steady
gestoßen, blurted out
get[eilt], divided (*divisi*)
getragen, solemn
gewichtig, heavy, weighty
gleichmäßig, equal, regular

(1te)(2te) Hälfte (zus[ammen]), the (1st) (2nd) half (together)
   (*unisono*)

im mäßigen Hauptzeitmaß, in a moderated basic tempo
immer (f) (stacc., etc.), always, steadily (*forte, staccato,* etc.)
immer bewegter im Vortrage, steadily more agitated in its execution
immer sehr ruhig (weich), always very calm (delicate, tender)

in Cis, in C-sharp [timpani tuning]
in 4 gleichstark besetzten Partien, in four sections of equal number

kräftig, strong, forcible
kurz, short

langsam (und schmachtend), slow (and languishing)
lebhaft, lively
leicht, lightly
leidenschaftlicher, more passionate, vehement

mäßig im Hauptzeitmaß, moderately in the basic tempo
mit Dämpf[er], muted

nach D, change to D [timpani tuning]
natürlich, in the normal way
noch bewegter, even more agitated
noch gebunden, aber sehr gehalten, still *legato,* but very controlled
nur 2, two only
nur die 1te Hälfte d. Kb., only the first half of the contrabasses

sämtl[iche], all together (*tutti*)
sehr, very
   [modifies numerous words in this glossary]
sehr kurz gestoßen, very short articulation ("outbursts")
   (*molto staccato*)
sehr mäßig beginnend (bewegt), very moderate at first
   (moving, agitated)

u[nd], and

von hier an sämtliche Violinen   from here on, all the violins
   nach der gewöhnlichen Ordnung   in the normal order of their
   der Pulte in 4 gleichen Partien   desks, in four equal parts
   [score note, *Lohengrin,* p. 154]

Vorspiel, prelude
wie vorher ♩. = ♩ [Literally, "the previous ♩. equals the present ♩"
   —but see p. 253, m. 6, for a more appropriate expression of the same
   metric equation in this context: ♩ ♩ ♩ = ♩ ♩]

zart, subdued, gentle
zu 2 = a2
zus[ammen], together (*unisono*)

Overtures and Preludes

Rienzi
der Letzte der Tribunen

[Rienzi, the Last of the Tribunes]

Tragic Opera in Five Acts

Libretto by Richard Wagner
after the blank-verse tragedy *Rienzi* (*ca.* 1828) by Mary Russell Mitford
and the novel *Rienzi* (1835) by Edward Bulwer-Lytton

Music by Richard Wagner

Score completed July 1837

First performance:
Königliches Hoftheater, Dresden
20 October 1842

Rienzi
Instrumentation

3 Flutes [Flauto]
    Fl. III doubles Piccolo [Flauto picc.]
2 Oboes [Oboe]
2 Clarinets in A [Clarinetto]
2 Bassoons [Fag(otto), Fg.]
Serpent* [Serpent]

4 Horns in F, A [Corno]
4 Trumpets in A [Tromba/i (*sic*), Trba.]
3 Trombones [Trombone/i, Trbne.]
Tuba [Tuba]

Timpani [Timpani]

Percussion:
    Snare Drum [Tamburo militare]
    Tenor Drum [Tamburo rollo]
    Triangle [Triangle]
    Bass Drum & Cymbals [Gran-cassa e Piatti]

Violins I, II [Violino, Viol.]
Violas [Viola]
Cellos [Violoncello, Vcl.]
Basses [Contrabasso]

*An obsolete woodwind, originally the keyless bass member of the early cornett family and the predecessor of the basshorn, Russian bassoon and ophicleide, employed as late as the early 19th century to support the bassoons.

Overture to
Rienzi
der Letzte der Tribunen
[Rienzi, the Last of the Tribunes]

Molto sostenuto e maestoso. ($\downarrow$=66)

Molto sostenuto e maestoso. ($\downarrow$=66)

NB. Zugleich für vereinfachte Besetzung, eingerichtet von Fritz Hoffmann. Bei kleiner Besetzung werden stets die in den Stimmen mit ∗ bezeichneten Noten der nicht vorhandenen Instrumente gespielt.

NB. Adapted for smaller Orchestras by Fritz Hoffmann. With small orchestras, the notes representing the absent instruments (indicated by ∗ in the parts) must be always played.

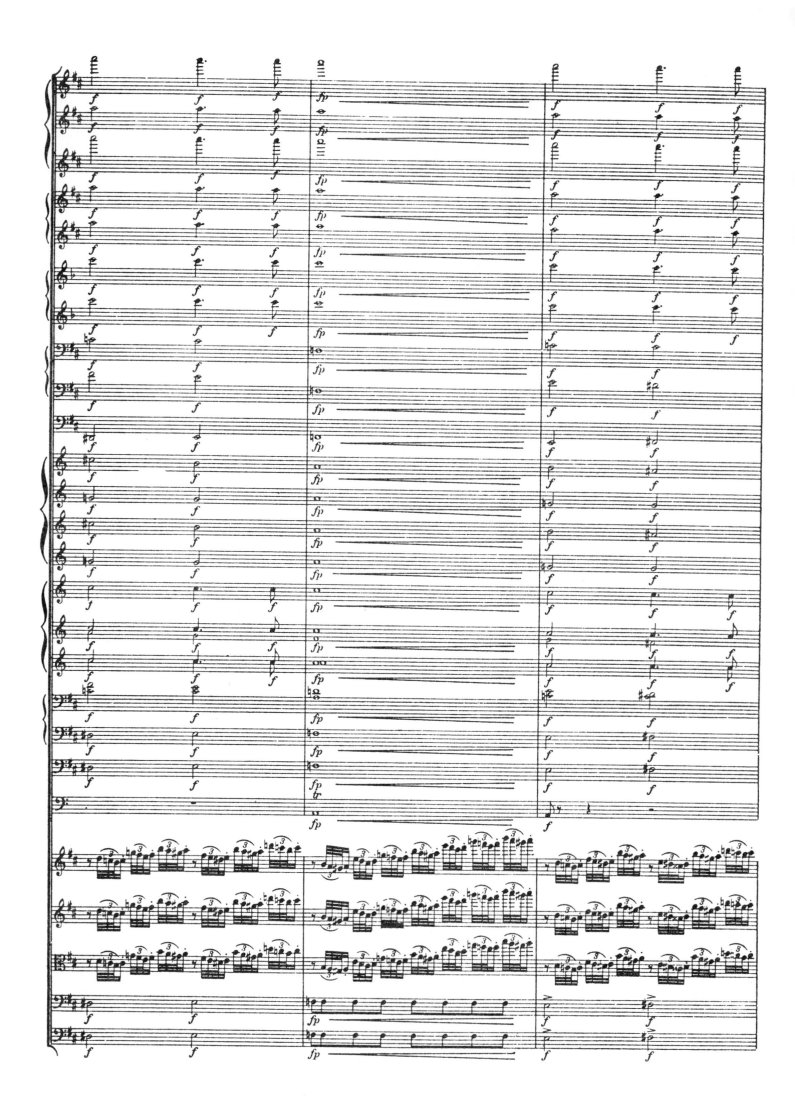

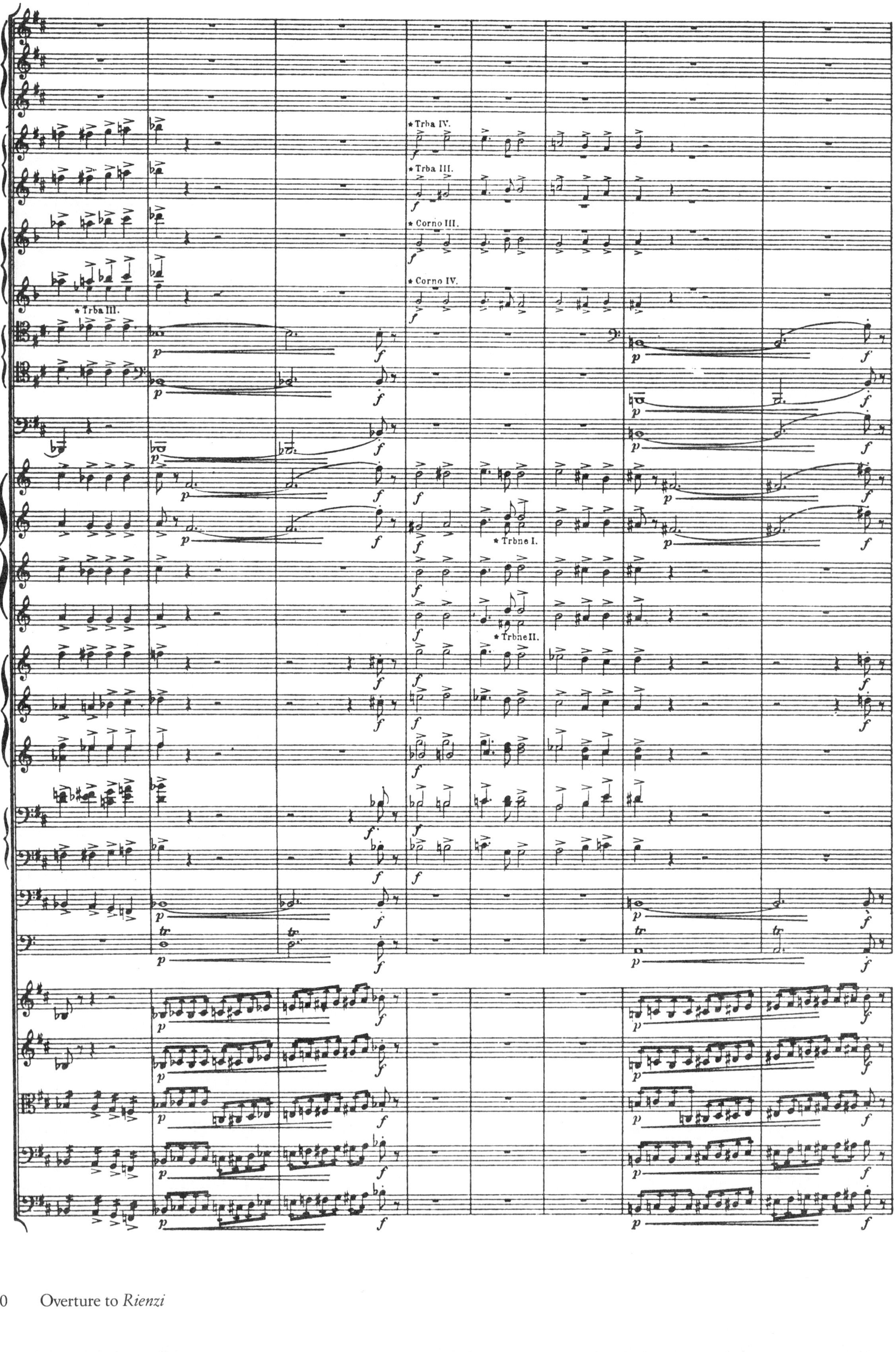
Trba IV.
Trba III.
Corno III.
Corno IV.
Trba III.
Trbne I.
Trbne II.

Molto più stretto. ($\mathbf{d}$=160.)

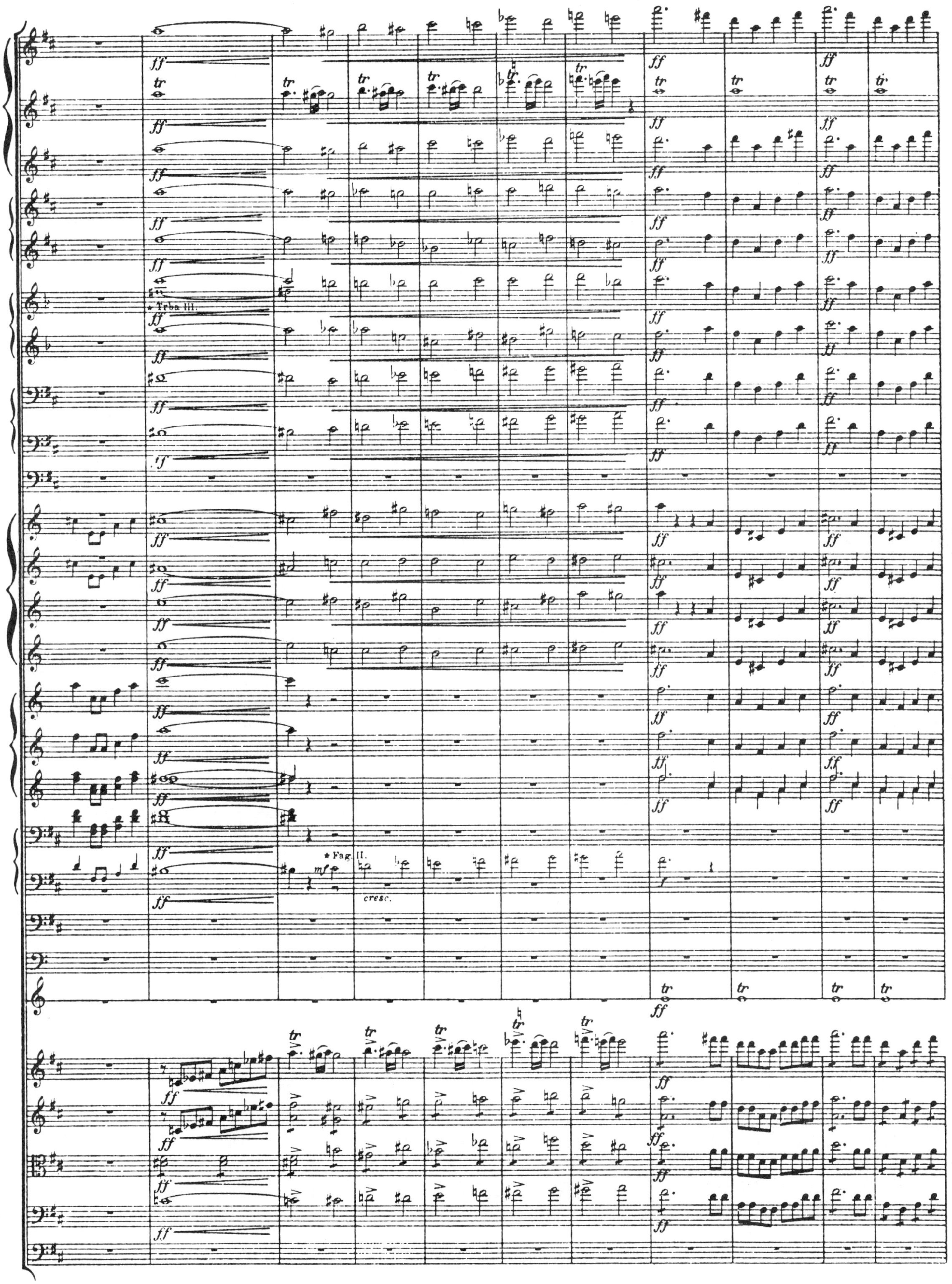
* Trba III.
* Fag. II.
mf
cresc.
ff
tr

Der fliegende Holländer

[The Flying Dutchman]

Romantic Opera in Three Acts

Libretto by Richard Wagner
after Heinrich Heine's "Aus den Memoiren des Herren von
Schnabelewopski" [From the Memoirs of Mr. Schnabelewopski]
(from *Der Salon* [The Drawing Room], vol. 1, 1834)

Music by Richard Wagner

Score (except the overture) completed October 1841
Overture completed November 1841
The final version of the complete work, reorchestrated in 1846,
includes revisions carried out in 1852 and 1860

First performance:
Königliches Hoftheater, Dresden
2 January 1843

Der fliegende Holländer
Instrumentation
Given in score order

Piccolo [Piccolo, Picc.]
2 Flutes [Flauti, Fl.]
2 Oboes [Oboi, Ob.]
2 Clarinets in C, B♭ [Clarinetti, Clar., Cl. (Ut, B/Si♭)]
English Horn [Corno ingl(ese)]

4 Horns in D, F, G, A [Corni, Cor. (Ré, Fa, Sol, La)]
2 Bassoons [Fagotti, Fag., Fg.]

2 Trumpets in D, F [Trombe/a, Tromb. (Ré, Fa)]
3 Trombones [Tromboni/e]
Tuba [Tuba]

Timpani [Timpani, Timp.]

Harp [Arpa]

Violins I, II [Violini, Viol., Vl.]
Violas [Viola]
Cellos [Violoncello, Vcll., Vcl., Vc.]
Basses [Contrabasso, Cb.]

Der fliegende Holländer

[The Flying Dutchman]

Overture to *Der fliegende Holländer*

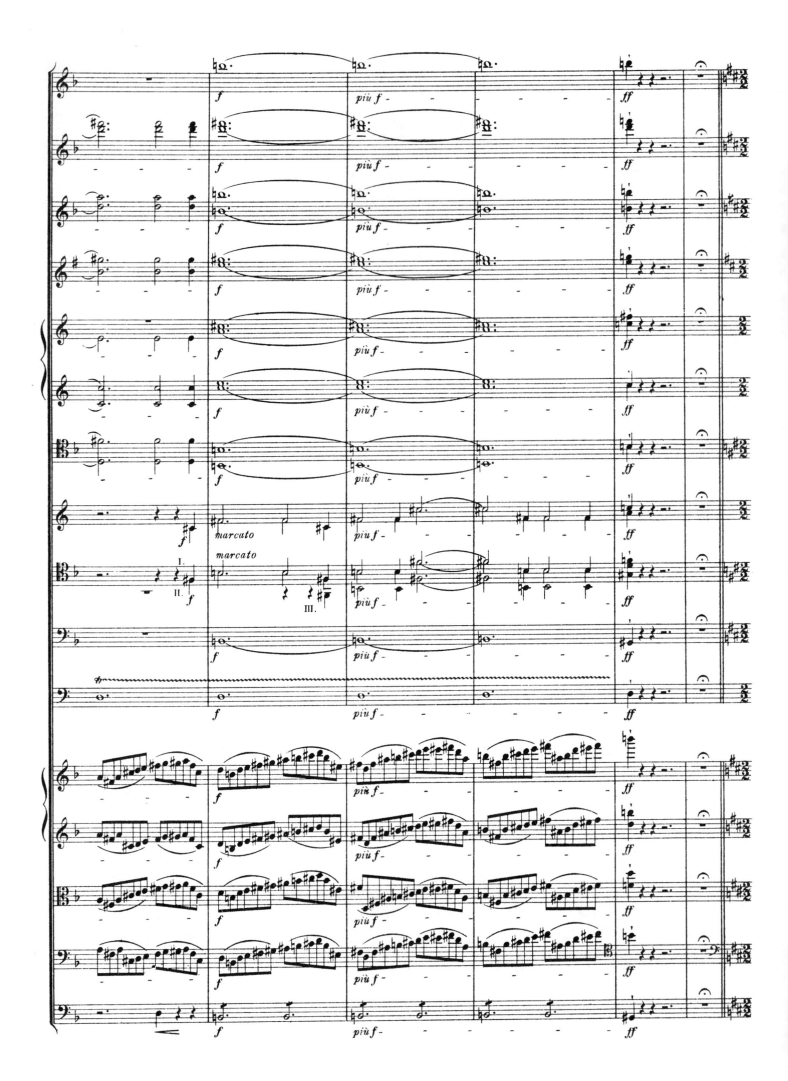

Tannhäuser
und der Sängerkrieg auf Wartburg

[Tannhäuser and the Singers' Contest at the Wartburg]

Romantic Opera in Three Acts

Libretto by Richard Wagner,
originally entitled *Der Venusberg* [Venus' Abode],
after the 13th-century legend preserved in the popular ballad *Danhauser* (1515)

Music by Richard Wagner

DRESDEN VERSION
Completed April 1845, revised 1845–6, 1847;
First performance: Königliches Hoftheater, Dresden, 19 October 1845

PARIS VERSION
A revision of the Dresden version
with additions in French, completed 1860–61;
First performance: Opéra, Paris, 13 March 1861

FINAL VERSION
Including German translations
of the French additions and revisions, completed 1865;
First performance: Königliches Hof- und Nationaltheater, Munich
5 March 1865

WITH NEW BRIDGE
From the overture to Act I, completed 1875;
First performance: Hofoper, Vienna, 22 November 1875

Tannhäuser
Instrumentation
Given in score order

Piccolo [kleine Flöte, kl. Fl.]
2 Flutes [große Flöten, gr. Fl.]
2 Oboes [Hoboen, Hb.]
2 Clarinets in A [Klarinetten, Kl.]

2 Valve Horns in E [Ventilhörner, Vh.]
2 Natural Horns in E [Waldhörner, Wh.]
2 Bassoons [Fagotte, Fg.]

3 Valve Trumpets in E [Ventiltrompeten, Vtrp.]
3 Trombones [Posaunen, Pos.]
    (2 Tenor-, 1 Baßposaune)
Bass Tuba [Baßtuba, Tba.]

Percussion:
    Triangle [Triangel, Trgl.]
    Cymbals [Becken, Bckn.]
    Tambourine [Tamburin, Tamb.]

Timpani [Pauken, Pk.]

Violins I, II [Violinen, Vl.]
Violas [Bratsche, Br.]
Cellos [Violoncell., Vc.]
Basses [Kontrabaß, Kb.]

Overture to
Tannhäuser
und der Sängerkrieg auf Wartburg
[Tannhäuser and the Singers' Contest at the Wartburg]

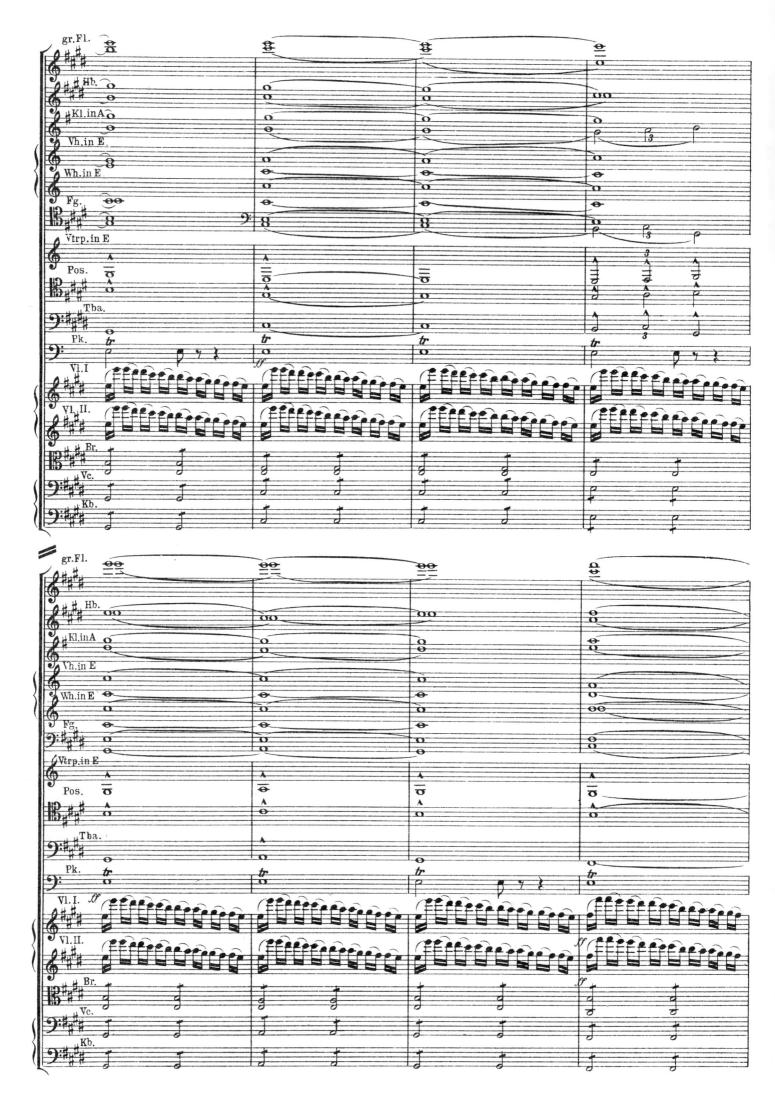

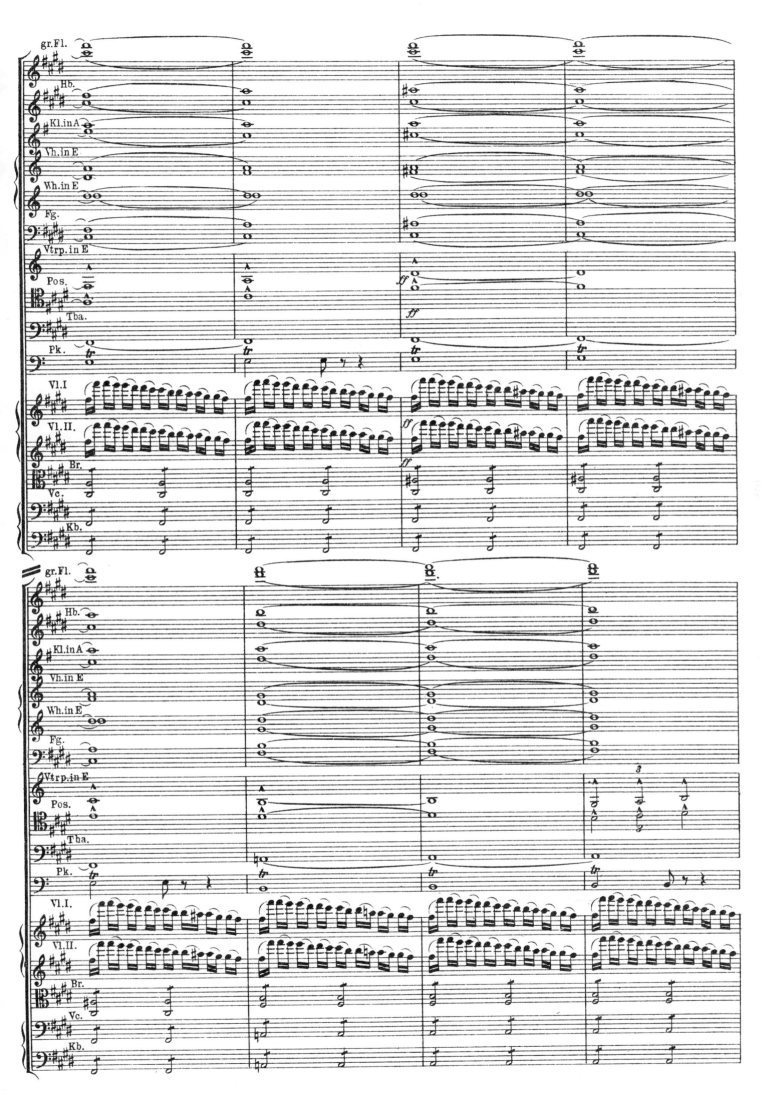

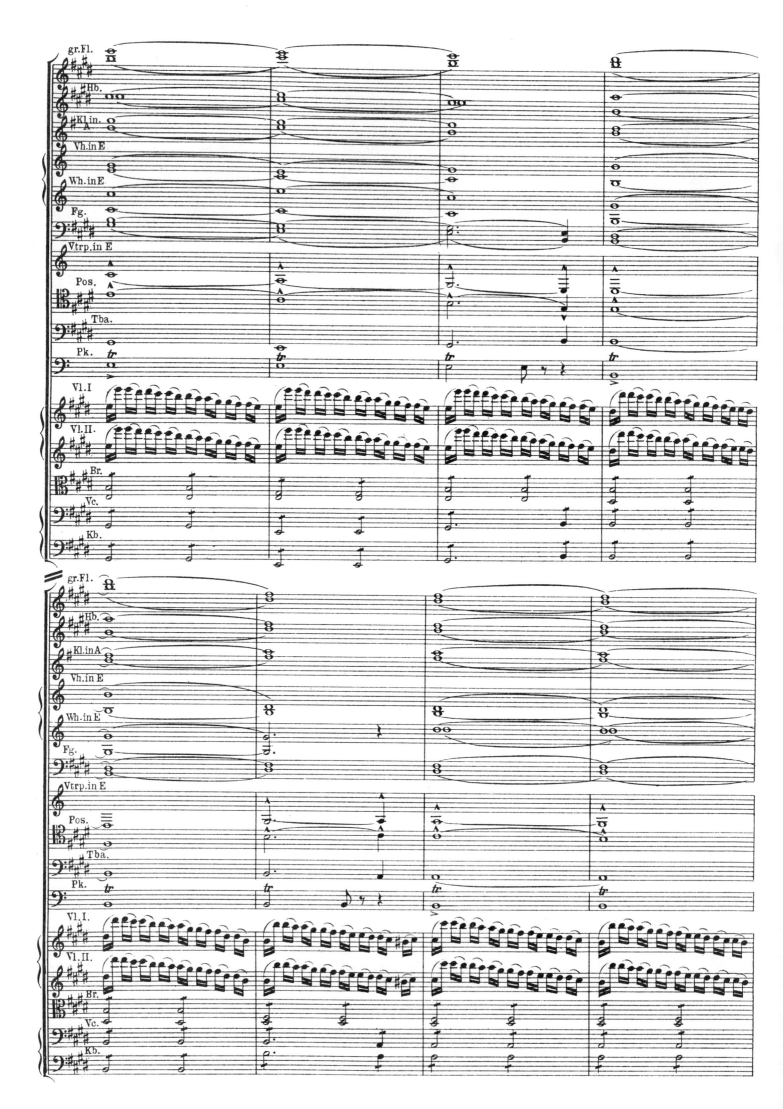

Lohengrin

Romantic Opera in Three Acts

Music and libretto by
Richard Wagner

Prose scenario and poem completed 1845,
revised during composition; score completed April 1848

First performance:
Hoftheater, Weimar
28 August 1850

Lohengrin (*ACT I*)

Instrumentation

Given in score order

3 Flutes [große Flöten, Fl.]
2 Oboes [Hoboen, Hb.]
English Horn [Englisch Horn, Engl. H.]
2 Clarinets in A [Klarinetten, Kl.]
Bass Clarinet in A [Baßklarinette, Bßkl.]
3 Bassoons [Fagotte, Fg.]

4 Horns in D, E [Hörner, Hr.]
3 Trumpets in C, D, E [Trompeten, Trp.]
3 Trombones [Posaunen, Pos.]
    (2 Tenor-, 1 Baßposaune)
Bass Tuba [Baßtuba, Tba.]

Timpani & Cymbals [Pauken (Pk.) und Becken (Bckn.)]

4 Solo Violins [4 einzelne Violinen, Viol., Vl.]
All other violins, in four sections of equal number
    [Sämtliche übrigen Violinen in 4 gleichstark besetzten Partien]
Violas [Bratsche, Br.]
Cellos [Violoncell., Vc.]
Basses [Kontrabaß, Kb.]

Lohengrin

★) Durch Flageolett hervorzubringen.

Lohengrin (*ACT III*)
Instrumentation
Given in score order

3 Flutes [Fls.]
3 Oboes [Obs.]
3 Clarinets in A [Cls.]
3 Bassoons [Bsns.]

4 Horns in D, E, G, A♭ [Hns.]
3 Trumpets in C, D, E♭, E [Tpts.]
3 Trombones [Tbns.]
Bass Tuba [Tuba]

Timpani [Timp.]
Triangle [Trgl.]
Cymbals [Cym.]
Tambourine [Tamb.]

Violins I, II [Vlns.]
Violas [Vla.]
Cellos [Vcl.]
Basses [B.]

Prelude to Act III of
Lohengrin

Tristan und Isolde

[Tristan and Iseult]

Tragic Opera in Three Acts

Libretto by Richard Wagner
after the medieval Celtic legend of Drystan and Essylt,
based on the narrative by the Anglo-Norman poet Thomas of Brittany
(*ca.* 1160) and its retelling by Gottfried von Strassburg (*ca.* 1210)

Music by Richard Wagner

Score completed August 1859

First performance:
Königliches Hof- und Nationaltheater, Munich
10 June 1865

Tristan und Isolde
Instrumentation
Given in score order

3 Flutes [Flöten, Fl.]
   Fl. III doubles Piccolo [klein Flöte, kl. Fl.]
2 Oboes [Hoboen, Hb.]
2 Clarinets in A [Klarinetten, Kl.]
English Horn [Englisch Horn, Engl. H.]

4 Horns in E, F [Hörner, Hr.]
3 Bassoons [Fagotte, Fg.]
Bass Clarinet in A [Baßklarinette, Bßkl.]

3 Trumpets in E, F [Trompeten, Trp.]
3 Trombones [Posaunen, Pos.]
   (2 Tenor-, 1 Baßposaune)
Bass Tuba [Baßtuba, Tba.]

Timpani [Pauken, Pk.]

Harp [Harfe, Hrfe.]

[Soprano Solo: "Isoldens Liebestod"]

Violins I, II [Violinen, Vl.]
Violas [Bratsche, Br.]
Cellos [Violoncell., Vc.]
Basses [Kontrabaß, Kb.]

Tristan und Isolde
Prelude and Liebestod

[Tristan and Iseult]
(Prelude and Love-Death / Vorspiel und Isoldens Liebestod)

Vorspiel.
Langsam und schmachtend.

Prelude & Liebestod from *Tristan und Isolde*

188   Prelude & Liebestod from *Tristan und Isolde*

Prelude & Liebestod from *Tristan und Isolde*

Isoldens Liebestod.
Sehr mäßig beginnend.

Prelude & Liebestod from *Tristan und Isolde*

Die Meistersinger von Nürnberg

[The Mastersingers of Nürnberg]

Opera in Three Acts

Music and libretto by Richard Wagner

Score completed October 1867

First performance:
Königliches Hof- und Nationaltheater, Munich
21 June 1868

Die Meistersinger
Instrumentation
Given in score order

Piccolo [kleine Flöte]
2 Flutes [große Flöten, gr. Fl.]
2 Oboes [Hoboen, Hb.]
2 Clarinets in B♭ [Klarinetten, Kl. (B)]
English Horn [Englisch Horn, Engl. H.]

4 Horns in C, F [Hörner, Hr.]
2 Bassoons [Fagotte, Fg.]

3 Trumpets in C, F [Trompeten, Trp.]
3 Trombones [Posaunen, Pos.]
 (2 Tenor-, 1 Baßposaune)
Bass Tuba [Baßtuba, Tba.]

Percussion:
 Triangle [Triangel, Trgl.]
 Cymbals [Becken, Bck.]

Timpani [Pauken, Pk.]

Harp [Harfe, Hrfe.]

Violins I, II [Violinen, Vl.]
Violas [Bratsche, Br.]
Cellos [Violoncell., Vc.]
Basses [Kontrabaß, Kb.]

Overture to
Die Meistersinger von Nürnberg
[The Mastersingers of Nürnberg]

Parsifal

("Bühnenweihfestspiel"*)

Opera in Three Acts

Libretto by Richard Wagner
based upon legends of the Grail, including Chrétien de Troyes'
Arthurian romance *Perceval, ou Le Conte du Graal* (before 1190),
the epic poem *Parzival* (*ca.* 1200–10) by Wolfram von Eschenbach,
and the so-called *Mabinogion* manuscript (14th c.)

Music by Richard Wagner

Score (Wagner's last work) completed January 1882

First performance:
Festspielhaus, Bayreuth
26 July 1882

*"Festival play for the dedication of the stage" [of Bayreuth's Festspielhaus, 1882].

Parsifal
Instrumentation

3 Flutes [Flöten, Fl.]
3 Oboes [Hoboen, Hb.]
English Horn [Althoboe, Althb.]
3 Clarinets in B♭ [Klarinetten, Kl. (B)]
*Bass Clarinet in B♭ [Baßklarinette (B)]
3 Bassoons [Fagotte, Fg.]
Contrabassoon [Kontrafag(ott)]

4 Horns in E, F [Hörner, Hr.]
3 Trumpets in F [Trompeten, Trp.]
3 Trombones [Posaunen, Pos.]
    (2 Tenor-, 1 Baßposaune)
Bass Tuba [Baßtuba, Tba.]

Timpani [Pauken, Pk.]

Violins I, II [Violinen, Vl.]
Violas [Bratsche, Br.]
Cellos [Violoncell., Vc.]
Basses [Kontrabaß, Kb.]

*Although a staff is provided for the bass clarinet, this instrument does not play in the Prelude.

Prelude to
Parsifal

sehr getragen.

Dover Orchestral Scores

THE SIX BRANDENBURG CONCERTOS AND THE FOUR ORCHESTRAL SUITES IN FULL SCORE, Johann Sebastian Bach. Complete standard Bach-Gesellschaft editions in large, clear format. Study score. 273pp. 9 × 12. 23376-6 Pa. **$11.95**

COMPLETE CONCERTI FOR SOLO KEYBOARD AND ORCHESTRA IN FULL SCORE, Johann Sebastian Bach. Bach's seven complete concerti for solo keyboard and orchestra in full score from the authoritative Bach-Gesellschaft edition. 206pp. 9 × 12. 24929-8 Pa. **$10.95**

THE THREE VIOLIN CONCERTI IN FULL SCORE, Johann Sebastian Bach. Concerto in A Minor, BWV 1041; Concerto in E Major, BWV 1042; and Concerto for Two Violins in D Minor, BWV 1043. Bach-Gesellschaft edition. 64pp. 9⅜ × 12¼. 25124-1 Pa. **$5.95**

GREAT ORGAN CONCERTI, OPP. 4 & 7, IN FULL SCORE, George Frideric Handel. 12 organ concerti composed by great Baroque master are reproduced in full score from the *Deutsche Handelgesellschaft* edition. 138pp. 9⅜ × 12¼. 24462-8 Pa. **$8.95**

COMPLETE CONCERTI GROSSI IN FULL SCORE, George Frideric Handel. Monumental Opus 6 Concerti Grossi, Opus 3 and "Alexander's Feast" Concerti Grossi—19 in all—reproduced from most authoritative edition. 258pp. 9⅜ × 12¼. 24187-4 Pa. **$12.95**

COMPLETE CONCERTI GROSSI IN FULL SCORE, Arcangelo Corelli. All 12 concerti in the famous late nineteenth-century edition prepared by violinist Joseph Joachim and musicologist Friedrich Chrysander. 240pp. 8⅜ × 11¼. 25606-5 Pa. **$12.95**

WATER MUSIC AND MUSIC FOR THE ROYAL FIREWORKS IN FULL SCORE, George Frideric Handel. Full scores of two of the most popular Baroque orchestral works performed today—reprinted from definitive Deutsche Handelgesellschaft edition. Total of 96pp. 8⅛ × 11. 25070-9 Pa. **$6.95**

LATER SYMPHONIES, Wolfgang A. Mozart. Full orchestral scores to last symphonies (Nos. 35-41) reproduced from definitive Breitkopf & Härtel Complete Works edition. Study score. 285pp. 9 × 12. 23052-X Pa. **$11.95**

17 DIVERTIMENTI FOR VARIOUS INSTRUMENTS, Wolfgang A. Mozart. Sparkling pieces of great vitality and brilliance from 1771–1779; consecutively numbered from 1 to 17. Reproduced from definitive Breitkopf & Härtel Complete Works edition. Study score. 241pp. 9⅜ × 12¼. 23862-8 Pa. **$11.95**

PIANO CONCERTOS NOS. 11–16 IN FULL SCORE, Wolfgang Amadeus Mozart. Authoritative Breitkopf & Härtel edition of six staples of the concerto repertoire, including Mozart's cadenzas for Nos. 12–16. 256pp. 9⅜ × 12¼. 25468-2 Pa. **$12.95**

PIANO CONCERTOS NOS. 17–22, Wolfgang Amadeus Mozart. Six complete piano concertos in full score, with Mozart's own cadenzas for Nos. 17–19. Breitkopf & Härtel edition. Study score. 370pp. 9⅜ × 12¼. 23599-8 Pa. **$14.95**

PIANO CONCERTOS NOS. 23–27, Wolfgang Amadeus Mozart. Mozart's last five piano concertos in full score, plus cadenzas for Nos. 23 and 27, and the Concert Rondo in D Major, K.382. Breitkopf & Härtel edition. Study score. 310pp. 9⅜ × 12¼. 23600-5 Pa. **$12.95**

CONCERTI FOR WIND INSTRUMENTS IN FULL SCORE, Wolfgang Amadeus Mozart. Exceptional volume contains ten pieces for orchestra and wind instruments and includes some of Mozart's finest, most popular music. 272pp. 9⅜ × 12¼. 25228-0 Pa. **$13.95**

THE VIOLIN CONCERTI AND THE SINFONIA CONCERTANTE, K.364, IN FULL SCORE, Wolfgang Amadeus Mozart. All five violin concerti and famed double concerto reproduced from authoritative Breitkopf & Härtel Complete Works Edition. 208pp. 9⅜ × 12½. 25169-1 Pa. **$11.95**

SYMPHONIES 88–92 IN FULL SCORE: The Haydn Society Edition, Joseph Haydn. Full score of symphonies Nos. 88 through 92. Large, readable noteheads, ample margins for fingerings, etc., and extensive Editor's Commentary. 304pp. 9 × 12. (Available in U.S. only) 24445-8 Pa. **$13.95**

COMPLETE LONDON SYMPHONIES IN FULL SCORE, Series I and Series II, Joseph Haydn. Reproduced from the Eulenburg editions are Symphonies Nos. 93–98 (Series I) and Nos. 99–104 (Series II). 800pp. 8⅜ × 11¼. (Available in U.S. only) Series I 24982-4 Pa. **$15.95** Series II 24983-2 Pa. **$16.95**

FOUR SYMPHONIES IN FULL SCORE, Franz Schubert. Schubert's four most popular symphonies: No. 4 in C Minor ("Tragic"); No. 5 in B-flat Major; No. 8 in B Minor ("Unfinished"); and No. 9 in C Major ("Great"). Breitkopf & Härtel edition. Study score. 261pp. 9⅜ × 12¼. 23681-1 Pa. **$12.95**

GREAT OVERTURES IN FULL SCORE, Carl Maria von Weber. Overtures to *Oberon, Der Freischutz, Euryanthe* and *Preciosa* reprinted from authoritative Breitkopf & Härtel editions. 112pp. 9 × 12. 25225-6 Pa. **$8.95**

SYMPHONIES NOS. 1, 2, 3, AND 4 IN FULL SCORE, Ludwig van Beethoven. Republication of H. Litolff edition. 272pp. 9 × 12. 26033-X Pa. **$10.95**

SYMPHONIES NOS. 5, 6 AND 7 IN FULL SCORE, Ludwig van Beethoven. Republication of the H. Litolff edition. 272pp. 9 × 12. 26034-8 Pa. **$10.95**

SYMPHONIES NOS. 8 AND 9 IN FULL SCORE, Ludwig van Beethoven. Republication of the H. Litolff edition. 256pp. 9 × 12. 26035-6 Pa. **$10.95**

SIX GREAT OVERTURES IN FULL SCORE, Ludwig van Beethoven. Six staples of the orchestral repertoire from authoritative Breitkopf & Härtel edition. *Leonore Overtures*, Nos. 1–3; Overtures to *Coriolanus, Egmont, Fidelio.* 288pp. 9 × 12. 24789-9 Pa. **$13.95**

COMPLETE PIANO CONCERTOS IN FULL SCORE, Ludwig van Beethoven. Complete scores of five great Beethoven piano concertos, with all cadenzas as he wrote them, reproduced from authoritative Breitkopf & Härtel edition. New table of contents. 384pp. 9⅜ × 12¼. 24563-2 Pa. **$14.95**

GREAT ROMANTIC VIOLIN CONCERTI IN FULL SCORE, Ludwig van Beethoven, Felix Mendelssohn and Peter Ilyitch Tchaikovsky. The Beethoven Op. 61, Mendelssohn, Op. 64 and Tchaikovsky, Op. 35 concertos reprinted from the Breitkopf & Härtel editions. 224pp. 9 × 12. 24989-1 Pa. **$10.95**

MAJOR ORCHESTRAL WORKS IN FULL SCORE, Felix Mendelssohn. Generally considered to be Mendelssohn's finest orchestral works, here in one volume are: the complete *Midsummer Night's Dream; Hebrides Overture; Calm Sea and Prosperous Voyage Overture;* Symphony No. 3 in A ("Scottish"); and Symphony No. 4 in A ("Italian"). Breitkopf & Härtel edition. Study score. 406pp. 9 × 12. 23184-4 Pa. **$16.95**

COMPLETE SYMPHONIES, Johannes Brahms. Full orchestral scores. No. 1 in C Minor, Op. 68; No. 2 in D Major, Op. 73; No. 3 in F Major, Op. 90; and No. 4 in E Minor, Op. 98. Reproduced from definitive Vienna Gesellschaft der Musikfreunde edition. Study score. 344pp. 9 × 12. 23053-8 Pa. **$13.95**

*Available from your music dealer or write for **free** Music Catalog to*
Dover Publications, Inc., Dept. MUBI, 31 East 2nd Street, Mineola, N.Y. 11501.

Dover Opera, Choral and Lieder Scores

ELEVEN GREAT CANTATAS, J. S. Bach. Full vocal-instrumental score from Bach-Gesellschaft edition. *Christ lag in Todesbanden, Ich hatte viel Bekümmerniss, Jauchhzet Gott in allen Landen,* eight others. Study score. 350pp. 9 × 12. 23268-9 Pa. **$14.95**

SEVEN GREAT SACRED CANTATAS IN FULL SCORE, Johann Sebastian Bach. Seven favorite sacred cantatas. Printed from a clear, modern engraving and sturdily bound; new literal line-for-line translations. Reliable Bach-Gesellschaft edition. Complete German texts. 256pp. 9 × 12. 24950-6 Pa. **$12.95**

SIX GREAT SECULAR CANTATAS IN FULL SCORE, Johann Sebastian Bach. Bach's nearest approach to comic opera. *Hunting Cantata, Wedding Cantata, Aeolus Appeased, Phoebus and Pan, Coffee Cantata,* and *Peasant Cantata.* 286pp. 9 × 12. 23934-9 Pa. **$13.95**

MASS IN B MINOR IN FULL SCORE, Johann Sebastian Bach. The crowning glory of Bach's lifework in the field of sacred music and a universal statement of Christian faith, reprinted from the authoritative Bach-Gesellschaft edition. Translation of texts. 320pp. 9 × 12. 25992-7 Pa. **$12.95**

GIULIO CESARE IN FULL SCORE, George Frideric Handel. Great Baroque masterpiece reproduced directly from authoritative Deutsche Handelgesellschaft edition. Gorgeous melodies, inspired orchestration. Complete and unabridged. 160pp. 9⅜ × 12¼. 25056-3 Pa. **$11.95**

MESSIAH IN FULL SCORE, George Frideric Handel. An authoritative full-score edition of the oratorio that is the best-known, most beloved, most performed large-scale musical work in the English-speaking world. 240pp. 9 × 12. 26067-4 Pa. **$11.95**

REQUIEM IN FULL SCORE, Wolfgang Amadeus Mozart. Masterpiece of vocal composition, among the most recorded and performed works in the repertoire. Authoritative edition published by Breitkopf & Härtel, Wiesbaden, n.d. 203pp. 8⅜ × 11¼. 25311-2 Pa. **$7.95**

COSI FAN TUTTE IN FULL SCORE, Wolfgang Amadeus Mozart. Scholarly edition of one of Mozart's greatest operas. Da Ponte libretto. Commentary. Preface. Translated frontmatter. 448pp. 9⅜ × 12¼. (Available in U.S. only) 24528-4 Pa. **$17.95**

THE MARRIAGE OF FIGARO: COMPLETE SCORE, Wolfgang A. Mozart. Finest comic opera ever written. Full score, not to be confused with piano renderings. Peters edition. Study score. 448pp. 9⅜ × 12¼. (Available in U.S. only) 23751-6 Pa. **$17.95**

DON GIOVANNI: COMPLETE ORCHESTRAL SCORE, Wolfgang A. Mozart. Full score, not to be confused with piano reductions. All optional numbers, much material not elsewhere. Peters edition. Study score. 468pp. 9⅜ × 12¼. (Available in U.S. only) 23026-0 Pa. **$19.95**

THE ABDUCTION FROM THE SERAGLIO IN FULL SCORE, Wolfgang Amadeus Mozart. Mozart's early comic masterpiece, exactingly reproduced from the authoritative Breitkopf & Härtel edition. 320pp. 9 × 12. 26004-6 Pa. **$12.95**

THE MAGIC FLUTE (DIE ZAUBERFLÖTE) IN FULL SCORE, Wolfgang Amadeus Mozart. Authoritative C. F. Peters edition of Mozart's last opera featuring all the spoken dialogue. Translation of German frontmatter. Dramatis personae. List of Numbers. 226pp. 9 × 12. 24783-X Pa. **$11.95**

THE SEASONS IN FULL SCORE, Joseph Haydn. A masterful coda to a prolific career, this brilliant oratorio—Haydn's last major work. Unabridged republication of the work as published by C. F. Peters, Leipzig, n.d. English translation of frontmatter. 320pp. 9 × 12. 25022-9 Pa. **$16.95**

FIDELIO IN FULL SCORE, Ludwig van Beethoven. Beethoven's only opera, complete in one affordable volume, including all spoken German dialogue. Republication of C. F. Peters, Leipzig edition. 272pp. 9 × 12. 24740-6 Pa. **$13.95**

THE BARBER OF SEVILLE IN FULL SCORE, Gioacchino Rossini. One of the greatest comic operas ever written, reproduced here directly from the authoritative score published by Ricordi. 464pp. 8⅜ × 11¼. 26019-4 Pa. **$16.95**

GERMAN REQUIEM IN FULL SCORE, Johannes Brahms. Definitive Breitkopf & Härtel edition of Brahms's greatest vocal work, fully scored for solo voices, mixed chorus and orchestra. 208pp. 9⅜ × 12¼. 25486-0 Pa. **$10.95**

REQUIEM IN FULL SCORE, Giuseppe Verdi. Immensely popular with choral groups and music lovers. Republication of edition published by C. F. Peters, Leipzig, n.d. Study score. 204pp. 9⅜ × 12¼. (Available in U.S. only) 23682-X Pa. **$10.95**

OTELLO IN FULL SCORE, Giuseppe Verdi. The penultimate Verdi opera, his tragic masterpiece. Complete unabridged score from authoritative Ricordi edition, with frontmatter translated. 576pp. 8¼ × 11. 25040-7 Pa. **$21.95**

FALSTAFF, Giuseppe Verdi. Verdi's last great work, first and only comedy. Complete unabridged score from original Ricordi edition. 480pp. 8⅜ × 11¼. 24017-7 Pa. **$17.95**

AÏDA IN FULL SCORE, Giuseppe Verdi. Verdi's most popular opera in an authoritative edition from G. Ricordi of Milan. 448pp. 9 × 12. 26172-7 Pa. **$17.95**

LA BOHÈME IN FULL SCORE, Giacomo Puccini. Authoritative Italian edition of one of the world's most beloved operas. English translations of list of characters and instruments. 416pp. 8⅜ × 11¼. 25477-1 Pa. **$16.95**

DER FREISCHÜTZ, Carl Maria von Weber. Full orchestral score to first Romantic opera, path-breaker for later developments, Wagner. Still very popular. Study score, including full spoken text. 203pp. 9 × 12. 23449-5 Pa. **$11.95**

CARMEN IN FULL SCORE, Georges Bizet. Complete, authoritative score of what is perhaps the world's most popular opera, in the version most commonly performed today, with recitatives by Ernest Guiraud. 574pp. 9 × 12. 25820-3 Pa. **$21.95**

DAS RHEINGOLD IN FULL SCORE, Richard Wagner. Complete score, clearly reproduced from authoritative B. Schott's edition. New translation of German frontmatter. 328pp. 9 × 12. 24925-5 Pa. **$14.95**

DIE WALKÜRE, Richard Wagner. Complete orchestral score of the most popular of the operas in the Ring Cycle. Reprint of the edition published in Leipzig by C. F. Peters, ca. 1910. Study score. 710pp. 8⅜ × 11¼. 23566-1 Pa. **$24.95**

SIEGFRIED IN FULL SCORE, Richard Wagner. *Siegfried,* third opera of Wagner's famous *Ring,* is reproduced from first edition (1876). 439pp. 9⅜ × 12¼. 24456-3 Pa. **$19.95**

GÖTTERDÄMMERUNG, Richard Wagner. Full operatic score available in U.S. for the first time. Reprinted directly from rare 1877 first edition. 615pp. 9⅜ × 12¼. 24250-1 Pa. **$24.95**

DIE MEISTERSINGER VON NÜRNBERG, Richard Wagner. Landmark in history of opera in complete vocal and orchestral score. Do not confuse with piano reduction. Peters, Leipzig edition. Study score. 823pp. 8⅜ × 11. 23276-X Pa. **$28.95**

---

*Available from your music dealer or write for **free** Music Catalog to*
Dover Publications, Inc., Dept. MUBI, 31 East 2nd Street, Mineola, N.Y. 11501.

Dover Opera, Choral and Lieder Scores

LOHENGRIN IN FULL SCORE, Richard Wagner. Wagner's most accessible opera. Reproduced from first engraved edition (Breitkopf & Härtel, 1887). 295pp. 9⅜ × 12¼. 24335-4 Pa. **$17.95**

TANNHAUSER IN FULL SCORE, Richard Wagner. Reproduces the original 1845 full orchestral and vocal score as slightly amended in 1847. Included is the ballet music for Act I written for the 1861 Paris production. 576pp. 8⅜ × 11¼. 24649-3 Pa. **$21.95**

TRISTAN UND ISOLDE, Richard Wagner. Full orchestral score with complete instrumentation. Study score. 655pp. 8⅛ × 11. 22915-7 Pa. **$24.95**

PARSIFAL IN FULL SCORE, Richard Wagner. Composer's deeply personal treatment of the legend of the Holy Grail, renowned for splendid music, glowing orchestration. C. F. Peters edition. 592pp. 8⅛ × 11. 25175-6 Pa. **$19.95**

THE FLYING DUTCHMAN IN FULL SCORE, Richard Wagner. Great early masterpiece reproduced directly from limited Weingartner edition (1896), incorporating Wagner's revisions. Text, stage directions in English, German, Italian. 432pp. 9⅜ × 12¼. 25629-4 Pa. **$19.95**

BORIS GODUNOV IN FULL SCORE (Rimsky-Korsakov Version), Modest Petrovich Moussorgsky. Russian operatic masterwork in most recorded, performed version. Authoritative Moscow edition. 784pp. 8⅜ × 11¼. 25321-X Pa. **$32.95**

PELLÉAS ET MÉLISANDE IN FULL SCORE, Claude Debussy. Reprinted from the E. Fromont (1904) edition, this volume faithfully reproduces the full orchestral-vocal score of Debussy's sole and enduring opera masterpiece. 416pp. 9 × 12. (Available in U.S. only) 24825-9 Pa. **$18.95**

SALOME IN FULL SCORE, Richard Strauss. Atmospheric color predominates in basic 20th-century work. Definitive Fürstner score, now extremely rare. 352pp. 9⅜ × 12¼. (Available in U.S. only) 24208-0 Pa. **$15.95**

DER ROSENKAVALIER IN FULL SCORE, Richard Strauss. First inexpensive edition of great operatic masterpiece, reprinted complete and unabridged from rare, limited Fürstner edition (1910) approved by Strauss. 528pp. 9⅜ × 12¼. (Available in U.S. only) 25498-4 Pa. **$24.95**

DER ROSENKAVALIER: VOCAL SCORE, Richard Strauss. Inexpensive edition reprinted directly from original Fürstner (1911) edition of vocal score. Verbal text, vocal line and piano "reduction." 448pp. 8⅜ × 11¼. (Available in U.S. only) 25501-8 Pa. **$16.95**

THE MERRY WIDOW: Complete Score for Piano and Voice in English, Franz Lehar. Complete score for piano and voice, reprinted directly from the first English translation (1907) published by Chappell & Co., London. 224pp. 8⅜ × 11¼. (Available in U.S. only) 24514-4 Pa. **$10.95**

THE AUTHENTIC GILBERT & SULLIVAN SONGBOOK, W. S. Gilbert, A. S. Sullivan. 92 songs, uncut, original keys, in piano renderings approved by Sullivan. 399pp. 9 × 12. 23482-7 Pa. **$15.95**

MADRIGALS: BOOK IV & V, Claudio Monteverdi. 39 finest madrigals with new English line-for-line literal translations of the poems facing the Italian text. 256pp. 8⅛ × 11. (Available in U.S. only) 25102-0 Pa. **$12.95**

COMPLETE SONG CYCLES, Franz Schubert. Complete piano, vocal music of *Die Schöne Müllerin, Die Winterreise, Schwanengesang.* Also Drinker English singing translations. Breitkopf & Härtel edition. 217pp. 9⅜ × 12¼. 22649-2 Pa. **$9.95**

SCHUBERT'S SONGS TO TEXTS BY GOETHE, Franz Schubert. Only one-volume edition of Schubert's Goethe songs from authoritative Breitkopf & Härtel edition, plus all revised versions. New prose translation of poems. 84 songs. 256pp. 9⅜ × 12¼. 23752-4 Pa. **$13.95**

59 FAVORITE SONGS, Franz Schubert. "Der Wanderer," "Ave Maria," "Hark, Hark, the Lark," and 56 other masterpieces of lieder reproduced from the Breitkopf & Härtel edition. 256pp. 9⅜ × 12¼. 24849-6 Pa. **$10.95**

SONGS FOR SOLO VOICE AND PIANO, Ludwig van Beethoven. 71 lieder, including "Adelaide," "Wonne der Wehmuth," "Die ehre Gottes aus der Natur," and famous cycle *An die ferne Geliebta.* Breitkopf & Härtel edition. 192pp. 9 × 12. 25125-X Pa. **$10.95**

SELECTED SONGS FOR SOLO VOICE AND PIANO, Robert Schumann. Over 100 of Schumann's greatest lieder, set to poems by Heine, Goethe, Byron, others. Breitkopf & Härtel edition. 248pp. 9⅜ × 12¼. 24202-1 Pa. **$12.95**

THIRTY SONGS, Franz Liszt. Selection of extremely worthwhile though not widely-known songs. Texts in French, German, and Italian, all with English translations. Piano, high voice. 144pp. 9 × 12. 23197-6 Pa. **$9.95**

OFFENBACH'S SONGS FROM THE GREAT OPERETTAS, Jacques Offenbach. Piano, vocal (French text) for 38 most popular songs: *Orphée, Belle Hélène, Vie Parisienne, Duchesse de Gérolstein,* others. 21 illustrations. 195pp. 9 × 12. 23341-3 Pa. **$10.95**

SONGS, 1880–1904, Claude Debussy. Rich selection of 36 songs set to texts by Verlaine, Baudelaire, Pierre Louys, Charles d'Orleans, others. 175pp. 9 × 12. 24131-9 Pa. **$8.95**

THE COMPLETE MÖRIKE SONGS, Hugo Wolf. Splendid settings of 53 poems by Eduard Mörike. "Der Tambour," "Elfenlied," "Verborganheit," 50 more. New prose translations. 208pp. 9⅜ × 12¼. 24380-X Pa. **$11.95**

SPANISH AND ITALIAN SONGBOOKS, Hugo Wolf. Total of 90 songs by great 19th-century master of the genre. Reprint of authoritative C. F. Peters edition. New Translations of German texts. 256pp. 9⅜ × 12¼. 26156-5 Pa. **$12.95**

SIXTY SONGS, Gabriel Fauré. "Clair de lune," "Apres un reve," "Chanson du pecheur," "Automne," and other great songs set for medium voice. Reprinted from French editions. 288pp. 8⅜ × 11. (Not available in France or Germany) 26534-X Pa. **$13.95**

FRENCH ART SONGS OF THE NINETEENTH-CENTURY, Philip Hale (ed.). 39 songs from romantic period by 18 composers: Berioz, Chausson, Debussy (six songs), Gounod, Massenet, Thomas, etc. For high voice, French text, English singing translation. 182pp. 9 × 12. (Not available in France or Germany) 23680-3 Pa. **$9.95**

COMPLETE SONGS FOR SOLO VOICE AND PIANO (two volumes), Johannes Brahms. A total of 113 songs in complete score by greatest lieder writer since Schubert. Volume I contains 15-song cycle Die Schone Magelone; Volume II famous "Lullaby." Total of 448pp. 9⅜ × 12¼. Volume I 23820-2 Pa. **$11.95**
Volume II 23821-0 Pa. **$11.95**

COMPLETE SONGS FOR SOLO VOICE AND PIANO: Series III, Johannes Brahms. 64 songs, published between 1877–86, including such favorites as "Geheimnis," "Alte Liebe," and "Vergebliches Standchen." 224pp. 9 × 12. 23822-9 Pa. **$11.95**

COMPLETE SONGS FOR SOLO VOICE AND PIANO: Series IV, Johannes Brahms. 120 songs that complete the Brahms song oeuvre and sensitive arrangements of 91 folk and traditional songs. 240pp. 9 × 12. 23823-7 Pa. **$11.95**

*Available from your music dealer or write for **free** Music Catalog to Dover Publications, Inc., Dept. MUBI, 31 East 2nd Street, Mineola, N.Y. 11501.*

Dover Opera, Choral and Lieder Scores

LOHENGRIN IN FULL SCORE, Richard Wagner. Wagner's most accessible opera. Reproduced from first engraved edition (Breitkopf & Härtel, 1887). 295pp. 9⅜ × 12¼. 24335-4 Pa. **$17.95**

TANNHAUSER IN FULL SCORE, Richard Wagner. Reproduces the original 1845 full orchestral and vocal score as slightly amended in 1847. Included is the ballet music for Act I written for the 1861 Paris production. 576pp. 8⅜ × 11¼. 24649-3 Pa. **$21.95**

TRISTAN UND ISOLDE, Richard Wagner. Full orchestral score with complete instrumentation. Study score. 655pp. 8⅜ × 11. 22915-7 Pa. **$24.95**

PARSIFAL IN FULL SCORE, Richard Wagner. Composer's deeply personal treatment of the legend of the Holy Grail, renowned for splendid music, glowing orchestration. C. F. Peters edition. 592pp. 8⅜ × 11. 25175-6 Pa. **$19.95**

THE FLYING DUTCHMAN IN FULL SCORE, Richard Wagner. Great early masterpiece reproduced directly from limited Weingartner edition (1896), incorporating Wagner's revisions. Text, stage directions in English, German, Italian. 432pp. 9⅜ × 12¼. 25629-4 Pa. **$19.95**

BORIS GODUNOV IN FULL SCORE (Rimsky-Korsakov Version), Modest Petrovich Moussorgsky. Russian operatic masterwork in most recorded, performed version. Authoritative Moscow edition. 784pp. 8⅜ × 11¼. 25321-X Pa. **$32.95**

PELLÉAS ET MÉLISANDE IN FULL SCORE, Claude Debussy. Reprinted from the E. Fromont (1904) edition, this volume faithfully reproduces the full orchestral-vocal score of Debussy's sole and enduring opera masterpiece. 416pp. 9 × 12. (Available in U.S. only) 24825-9 Pa. **$18.95**

SALOME IN FULL SCORE, Richard Strauss. Atmospheric color predominates in basic 20th-century work. Definitive Fürstner score, now extremely rare. 352pp. 9⅜ × 12¼. (Available in U.S. only) 24208-0 Pa. **$15.95**

DER ROSENKAVALIER IN FULL SCORE, Richard Strauss. First inexpensive edition of great operatic masterpiece, reprinted complete and unabridged from rare, limited Fürstner edition (1910) approved by Strauss. 528pp. 9⅜ × 12¼. (Available in U.S. only) 25498-4 Pa. **$24.95**

DER ROSENKAVALIER: VOCAL SCORE, Richard Strauss. Inexpensive edition reprinted directly from original Fürstner (1911) edition of vocal score. Verbal text, vocal line and piano "reduction." 448pp. 8⅜ × 11¼. (Available in U.S. only) 25501-8 Pa. **$16.95**

THE MERRY WIDOW: Complete Score for Piano and Voice in English, Franz Lehar. Complete score for piano and voice, reprinted directly from the first English translation (1907) published by Chappell & Co., London. 224pp. 8⅜ × 11¼. (Available in U.S. only) 24514-4 Pa. **$10.95**

THE AUTHENTIC GILBERT & SULLIVAN SONGBOOK, W. S. Gilbert, A. S. Sullivan. 92 songs, uncut, original keys, in piano renderings approved by Sullivan. 399pp. 9 × 12. 23482-7 Pa. **$15.95**

MADRIGALS: BOOK IV & V, Claudio Monteverdi. 39 finest madrigals with new English line-for-line literal translations of the poems facing the Italian text. 256pp. 8⅜ × 11. (Available in U.S. only) 25102-0 Pa. **$12.95**

COMPLETE SONG CYCLES, Franz Schubert. Complete piano, vocal music of *Die Schöne Müllerin, Die Winterreise, Schwanengesang.* Also Drinker English singing translations. Breitkopf & Härtel edition. 217pp. 9⅜ × 12¼. 22649-2 Pa. **$9.95**

SCHUBERT'S SONGS TO TEXTS BY GOETHE, Franz Schubert. Only one-volume edition of Schubert's Goethe songs from authoritative Breitkopf & Härtel edition, plus all revised versions. New prose translation of poems. 84 songs. 256pp. 9⅜ × 12¼. 23752-4 Pa. **$13.95**

59 FAVORITE SONGS, Franz Schubert. "Der Wanderer," "Ave Maria," "Hark, Hark, the Lark," and 56 other masterpieces of lieder reproduced from the Breitkopf & Härtel edition. 256pp. 9⅜ × 12¼. 24849-6 Pa. **$10.95**

SONGS FOR SOLO VOICE AND PIANO, Ludwig van Beethoven. 71 lieder, including "Adelaide," "Wonne der Wehmuth," "Die ehre Gottes aus der Natur," and famous cycle *An die ferne Geliebta.* Breitkopf & Härtel edition. 192pp. 9 × 12. 25125-X Pa. **$10.95**

SELECTED SONGS FOR SOLO VOICE AND PIANO, Robert Schumann. Over 100 of Schumann's greatest lieder, set to poems by Heine, Goethe, Byron, others. Breitkopf & Härtel edition. 248pp. 9⅜ × 12¼. 24202-1 Pa. **$12.95**

THIRTY SONGS, Franz Liszt. Selection of extremely worthwhile though not widely-known songs. Texts in French, German, and Italian, all with English translations. Piano, high voice. 144pp. 9 × 12. 23197-6 Pa. **$9.95**

OFFENBACH'S SONGS FROM THE GREAT OPERETTAS, Jacques Offenbach. Piano, vocal (French text) for 38 most popular songs: *Orphée, Belle Héléne, Vie Parisienne, Duchesse de Gérolstein,* others. 21 illustrations. 195pp. 9 × 12. 23341-3 Pa. **$10.95**

SONGS, 1880–1904, Claude Debussy. Rich selection of 36 songs set to texts by Verlaine, Baudelaire, Pierre Louys, Charles d'Orleans, others. 175pp. 9 × 12. 24131-9 Pa. **$8.95**

THE COMPLETE MÖRIKE SONGS, Hugo Wolf. Splendid settings of 53 poems by Eduard Mörike. "Der Tambour," "Elfenlied," "Verborganheit," 50 more. New prose translations. 208pp. 9⅜ × 12¼. 24380-X Pa. **$11.95**

SPANISH AND ITALIAN SONGBOOKS, Hugo Wolf. Total of 90 songs by great 19th-century master of the genre. Reprint of authoritative C. F. Peters edition. New Translations of German texts. 256pp. 9⅜ × 12¼. 26156-5 Pa. **$12.95**

SIXTY SONGS, Gabriel Fauré. "Clair de lune," "Apres un reve," "Chanson du pecheur," "Automne," and other great songs set for medium voice. Reprinted from French editions. 288pp. 8⅜ × 11. (Not available in France or Germany) 26534-X Pa. **$13.95**

FRENCH ART SONGS OF THE NINETEENTH-CENTURY, Philip Hale (ed.). 39 songs from romantic period by 18 composers: Berioz, Chausson, Debussy (six songs), Gounod, Massenet, Thomas, etc. For high voice, French text, English singing translation. 182pp. 9 × 12. (Not available in France or Germany) 23680-3 Pa. **$9.95**

COMPLETE SONGS FOR SOLO VOICE AND PIANO (two volumes), Johannes Brahms. A total of 113 songs in complete score by greatest lieder writer since Schubert. Volume I contains 15-song cycle Die Schone Magelone; Volume II famous "Lullaby." Total of 448pp. 9⅜ × 12¼. Volume I 23820-2 Pa. **$11.95** Volume II 23821-0 Pa. **$11.95**

COMPLETE SONGS FOR SOLO VOICE AND PIANO: Series III, Johannes Brahms. 64 songs, published between 1877–86, including such favorites as "Geheimnis," "Alte Liebe," and "Vergebliches Standchen." 224pp. 9 × 12. 23822-9 Pa. **$11.95**

COMPLETE SONGS FOR SOLO VOICE AND PIANO: Series IV, Johannes Brahms. 120 songs that complete the Brahms song oeuvre and sensitive arrangements of 91 folk and traditional songs. 240pp. 9 × 12. 23823-7 Pa. **$11.95**

Available from your music dealer or write for free Music Catalog to
Dover Publications, Inc., Dept. MUBI, 31 East 2nd Street, Mineola, N.Y. 11501.